FLAGS FLYING

FLAGS FLYING

Patrick Ward

Introduction by Philip Norman

Gordon Fraser   London   1977

1-4-78 First published 1977 by
The Gordon Fraser Gallery Ltd., London and Bedford
Photographs copyright © Patrick Ward 1977
Introduction copyright © The Gordon Fraser Gallery 1977
ISBN 0 86092 000 3
Printed in Great Britain by Westerham Press, Westerham, Kent
Designed by Peter Guy

In 1953 I was 10 years old. All things then seemed to last for ever, including the Coronation of Elizabeth II. I lived in Ryde, Isle of Wight, and spent my days at the end of the pier where my father operated the pleasure pavilion. His premises included a restaurant with windows commanding an unrivalled view of the Fleet drawn up at Spithead for review. An even better vantage-point was the high platform around the dome, upon which, in the mornings, an artist sat at his easel, painting the Fleet and Spithead and the extremities of the pierhead railway terminus. I would stand beside him, numb with envy as his narrow brush touched in white lifebelts on the warships that lay like ranks of grey fish far out in the hot sea haze.

I grew sated with heat and strawberries and obligatory patriotism, and bored with boat trips around the Fleet. For souvenirs I received a circular Coronation jigsaw puzzle, a plastic rectangle of newly-minted Elizabethan coins, a semi-precious spoon and, from our pious Junior School head-mistress, a sky blue, Royal monogrammed copy of the Gospel According to St John. I prayed for our young Queen on the eve of the Coronation and, on the day itself, watching the ceremony on someone else's television, I felt a vague hope that some hitch would occur.

My instinct at the approach of the 1977 Silver Jubilee was to ignore it. The 25 years since I squandered my new Elizabethan coins had, if any-thing, diminished my taste for English ceremonial. Royal occasions are always used by the government of the day to divert our attention from some political mess or other. I noted the manufacture of Jubilee T-shirts and the imminence of Jubilee 'sales'. Then one evening, I happened to pass by a certain little street in Paddington, close to my home. It was a little street which had previously seemed to be awaiting demolition. Now I saw flags in it. There were small flags strung across it and larger flags draped from windows which did, after all, belong to someone. Auda-ciously cheerful, impudently patriotic, flags gleamed by the hundred in a curry-smelling Paddington sunset.

Journalism played its part in forcing the Jubilee on my attention. The night I saw the flags, I said to a friend, 'I hope they don't send me to cover the Queen's Scottish tour.' Two days later at dawn, there I was being thrown off the sleeper at Perth station. Journalism is like that.

In Scotland I became pro-Jubilee. My initiation was gentle enough, beginning with the sight of carpet being Hoovered on the goods platform where the Royal train would stop, and of the train's stopping-place being measured to a centimetre. I seem to remember, in the constricted space, holding my breath lest it should sully the brilliant flank of the Royal limousine. I remember the purple nose of the Royal chauffeur, and the little trapdoor through which he poked the Royal Standard. Of the dignitaries assembled to meet the train, I particularly remember the chairman of the Tayside Council, who wore a sporran hanging down in three parts like a pawnbroker's sign. These preparations aroused in me what I now recognise as the stirrings of patriotic love. I hoped that the Queen would decide to have a headache and stay away.

 She did no such thing, of course. Her train arrived, accurate to the second and the centimetre; she stepped down from it upon the carpet as required. How shy she looked, and how determined. How lightly she walked, as if on two private cushions of air. How dreadfully pink her coat was, throwing Prince Philip into a pink shadow to match his sardonic smile. This, chronologically speaking, was when the Jubilee took wing – when the Queen drove out of Perth station goods-yard into cheering streets that seemed to have been transported intact from the days of the Empire. I remember that, along a stretch of dual carriageway on the Dundee Road, a line of tree trunks spelt 'Long Live Our Noble Queen' and a plum-grower had put a notice outside his gate promising 'Victorias will be sent when ready'.

It might seem strange that we should express our love for the Queen by subjecting her to a Silver Jubilee – by compelling her to visit North Sea oilfields and to drive in state through Wembley when a more fitting gesture of gratitude would have been to allow her to go horse-racing in peace. The answer, of course, is that the Queen was the last person for whom the Jubilee was originally intended. It was intended for smug politicians and fatuous civic officials. It was intended for pompousness and dullness and repetition and empty rhetoric. It was intended to stimulate the manufacturers, poised in awesome array to show this country at its shabbiest. There were the Jubilee 'sales' and the Jubilee T-shirts – symbols, respectively, of our gullibility and conformism. There was the effusion of medallions, salvers, cutlery and tankards; of posters, pamphlets, car-stickers, novelty lollipops, tourists, BBC broadcasts, brochures and best-selling biographies; and of anti-Jubilee campaigns waged by sparsely-read literary papers in terms no less vaporous, self-indulgent and dull.

Despite the efforts of these multitudes, the Jubilee contrived to turn itself into a true celebration. It proved how something essentially false and stage-managed may be transformed and lifted up by one single stray atom of human spontaneity. It became one of those moments, not normally expected in peacetime, which reveal the British at their best – ingenious, exuberant, deprived of all inhibition and slightly mad. It was, in countless small ways, an uprising against the forces which have conspired to disconcert us as a nation. For a little while we put aside our paranoia and put on funny hats; we shut our insecurity in the coal-house and, against all evidence, determined to be cheerful again; even neighbourly.

The photographs in this book were never intended to be a comprehensive pictorial record of Britain during the Jubilee. They are, first of all, the work of a talented, inquisitive photographer, responsive to human extravagance and eccentricity howsoever such qualities may occur. Patrick Ward's approach was to shun the official pageantry, recorded so tenaciously by his fellow photographers, and instead to concentrate his attention on activities in two small streets in the Hammersmith area, Mirabel Road and Prothero Road, during the week of preparation that culminated in open-air street parties on Jubilee Day itself.

The simplicity of this idea has resulted in an essay better than I have yet seen, in pictures or words, on the British at a unique and fleeting moment of happy inspiration. Prothero Road and Mirabel Road possibly have less reason than most to feel joyful about anything. And yet the joy and zest and open-heartedness, the bare-faced, or red-and-white faced, patriotism captured by Ward's photographs were no less than at tens of thousands of similar celebrations throughout the country as Britons, of all classes and complexions, discovered one emotion, at least, in which they could truly believe.

There is a photograph by the great Frenchman Henri Cartier-Bresson, taken during the Coronation of George VI in 1937. It shows a row of people sitting along the base of a Trafalgar Square lion, raptly watching the procession pass while, under their dangling feet, a lone figure sleeps blissfully on a bed of litter. For me, the photographs taken by Patrick Ward in Mirabel Road, Prothero Road and elsewhere have something of similar charm, transcending mere novelty and occasion.

Philip Norman
London, July 1977

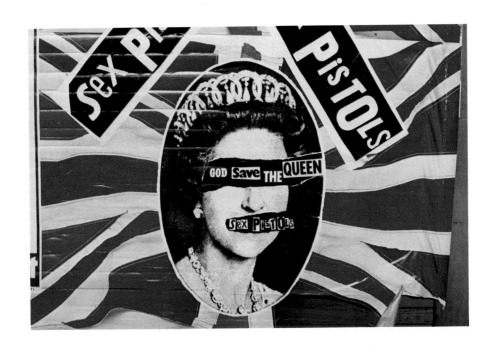